CLASSIC POP SONGS

TENOR SAX

Audio arrangements by Peter Deneff

To access audio visit:
www.halleonard.com/mylibrary
Enter Code
2353-1165-9777-9260

ISBN 978-1-5400-0246-4

HAL•LEONARD®

7777 W. BLUEMOUND RD. P.O. BOX 13819 MILWAUKEE, WI 53213

Visit Hal Leonard Online at
www.halleonard.com

BRIDGE OVER TROUBLED WATER

TENOR SAX

Words and Music by
PAUL SIMON

CANDLE IN THE WIND

TENOR SAX

Words and Music by ELTON JOHN
and BERNIE TAUPIN

Moderate Ballad

DUST IN THE WIND

TENOR SAX

Words and Music by
KERRY LIVGREN

5

EVERY BREATH YOU TAKE

TENOR SAX

Music and Lyrics by
STING

FIRE AND RAIN

TENOR SAX

Words and Music by
JAMES TAYLOR

HAVE I TOLD YOU LATELY

TENOR SAX

Words and Music by
VAN MORRISON

GOOD VIBRATIONS

TENOR SAX

Words and Music by BRIAN WILSON
and MIKE LOVE

HEAVEN

TENOR SAX

Words and Music by BRYAN ADAMS
and JIM VALLANCE

13

LEAN ON ME

TENOR SAX

Words and Music by
BILL WITHERS

15

SHE'S ALWAYS A WOMAN

TENOR SAX

Words and Music by
BILLY JOEL

WITH A LITTLE HELP FROM MY FRIENDS

TENOR SAX

Words and Music by JOHN LENNON
and PAUL McCARTNEY

TEARS IN HEAVEN

TENOR SAX

Words and Music by ERIC CLAPTON
and WILL JENNINGS